Dedicated To:
Natalie

Written By: Abigail Gartland

Hello, my name is St. Mother Teresa!

I was born in 1910 in the Ottoman Empire.

When I was only 12 years old, I knew I was called to serve God!

When I was 18, I said goodbye to my mom and dad, and joined the sisterhood!

I spent one year in Ireland and then went to India!

In India, I taught young people and became the principal of a school!

I spent my days teaching and loving all of the kids!

After several years, I felt God calling me to help people in a different way.

I lived in the poorest area of Calcutta, India, helping people who needed help the most.

When I helped people, I loved them like Jesus does.

We cannot all do big things to help people, but we all can do small things with great love.

What are some small things that you can do?

You can start by saying hello to someone!

You can also make sure that you are share with others!

You can help your family with the chores.

You can celebrate my feast day with me on September 5th!

I pray for you every day of your life.

St. Mother Teresa, Pray for Us!

Copyright:

Clipart: © PentoolPixie © LimeandKiwiDesigns
Licensed purchased: 1/10/2024

About the Author

Abigail Gartland

I love the saints and I love my faith. The idea for sharing the stories of the saints with little ones came when my dear friends were expecting their first baby. I wanted to create something as unique and special as our friendship. Each book is dedicated to very special people and groups who have enriched my faith in different ways. I am blessed to write these stories and appreciate the unending support of my family and friends. When I am not writing, am a middle school teacher. I hope you enjoy these stories. I pray for each and every person who opens one of my books to learn more about the saints.

Abbie

www.ingramcontent.com/pod-product-compliance
Lightning Source LLC
LaVergne TN
LVHW051042070526
838201LV00067B/4891